GRUMPY CAT'S

ALL ABOUT

MISERABLE

me

A Doodle Journal for Everything Awful

Jimi Bonogofsky-Gronseth

Dover Publications, Inc.
Mineola, New York

It's the face that has launched a thousand quips! Internet sensation Grumpy Cat® wants to get to know you, and here's your chance! Inside this miserable book you will find sixty-two pages in which you will get to tell Grumpy Cat the grossest foods, what superpower you would possess, and even what the monster under your bed looks like! Plus, you get to draw, doodle, and even solve some puzzles. And best of all——you get to hang out with Grumpy Cat!

Grumpy Cat™

Bibliographical Note

Grumpy Cat's All About Miserable Me: A Doodle Journal for Everything Awful
is a new work, first published by Dover Publications, Inc., in 2016.

International Standard Book Number

ISBN-13: 978-0-486-80744-7
ISBN-10: 0-486-80744-4

Manufactured in the United States by RR Donnelley
80744401   2016
www.doverpublications.com

Make a list of the
GROSSEST
FOODS.

1. _____

2. _____

3. _____

4. _____

5. _____

LOVE is a strong word.
Draw **3 PEOPLE** you
sorta KINDA like.

DRAW the UGLIEST sweater.

BEDHEAD
is the worst.
Draw what I look like in the MORNING.

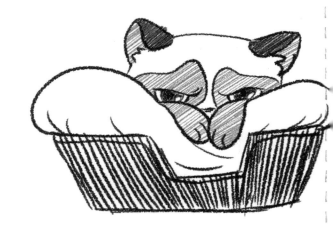

My
WORST
vacation.

I'm DONE with earth.
What should my
ROCKET SHIP
look like?

Now draw the
PLANET
I should go to.

The inhabitants of this planet
are all GRUMPY, LIKE ME.

Draw the
GRUMPY ALIENS.

Draw an
OUTFIT
on me.

I WON'T LIKE IT.

Thanks for the
TERRIBLE
birthday present.
What's inside?

Everyone needs an enemy.
Here's my ARCHENEMY.

You could even have a SUPERPOWER.
It wouldn't be as COOL as mine,
but WHAT would it be?

Everything makes me GRUMPY.
Be grumpy with me.
What makes YOU grumpy?

_____

_____

_____

_____

_____

_____

_____

I NEVER stop to
SMELL THE FLOWERS.
Draw me some flowers to IGNORE.

What does your completely SUBPAR PET look like?

Monsters are REAL.
What does the monster
UNDER YOUR BED
look like?

My trophy is for the
GRUMPIEST CAT EVER.
What is YOURS for?

name &
decorate
your trophy

If I made
HEADLINES,
what would the article be TITLED?

My headline

My article

SPORTS are way TOO MUCH WORK...
If you had to join a team,
what would you CALL it?

Create a
TERRIBLE MASCOT
for your sports team.

What are
THREE MASCOTS
that are WORSE than
the one you made?

Ugh... I don't feel so good.
I must have EATEN something bad...
Draw what's
INSIDE MY STOMACH.

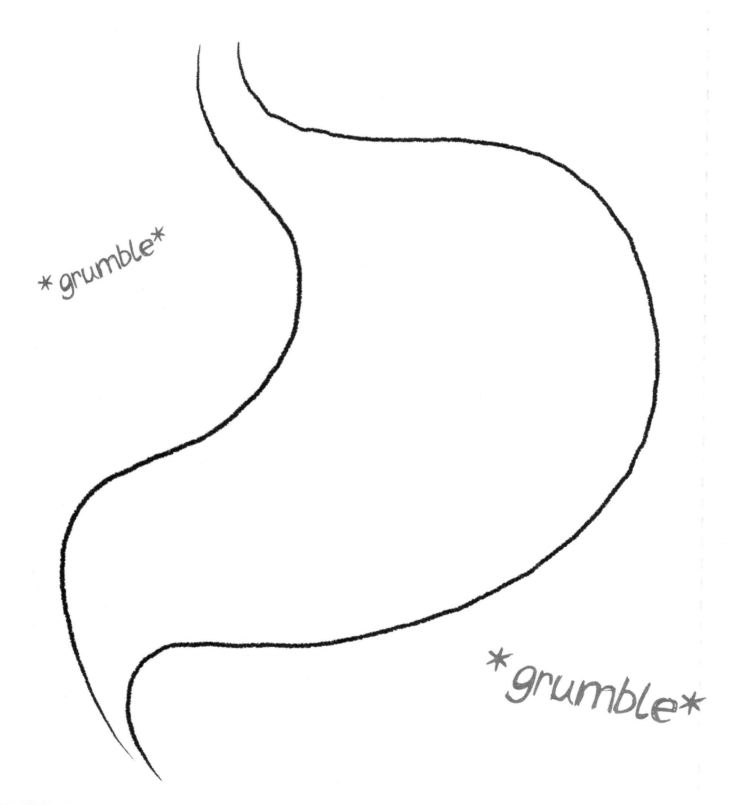

grumble

grumble

What should I name the
TITLE OF MY MEMOIR?

decorate my room

Draw your family as cats.
GRUMPY CATS.

Observe my gloriously
GRUMPY FACE
for inspiration.

I'm bored, so I'm going to
JOIN THE CIRCUS.
What am I BALANCING?

How can I make this
TRICK MORE DANGEROUS?

I guess I'm a WIZARD now.
What is my
FAVORITE SPELL?

Following this rainbow
was a TERRIBLE idea.

What did I find at the
OTHER SIDE?

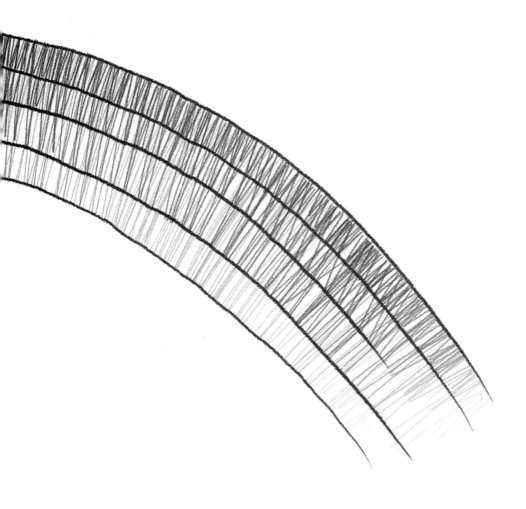

There is only ONE SPOT
in the house I like.

WHAT IS IT?

Pokey wants to start a BAND.
It's a TERRIBLE idea.
DRAW OUR INSTRUMENTS.

Try DRAWING ME with your
EYES CLOSED.

This is going to be AWFUL.

Anagrams are a way to
WASTE TIME for people who
THINK TOO MUCH.
Make an ANAGRAM out of my name.

G

R

U

M

P

Y

C

A

T

I'm writing a book called

MY VERY GRUMPY _____

Fill in the blank, then DRAW THE COVER
(so I don't have to).

Write me a HAIKU
Which PRAISES my grumpiness.
Just don't MESS IT UP.

(haikus are poems with 3 lines of
specific syllables lengths: 5, 7, 5)

Draw yourself as an
OLD PERSON.

I bet you'll have SO MANY wrinkles.

Your BEST FRIEND would probably prefer
to hang out with ME.
DRAW YOUR BFF
with me, instead.

Being royalty would probably be a HUGE PAIN.
But the CROWN might be okay.
DRAW MY CROWN.
(and make sure you're not stingy with the jewels)

I'm grumpy even when I SLEEP.
What am I
DREAMING
about?

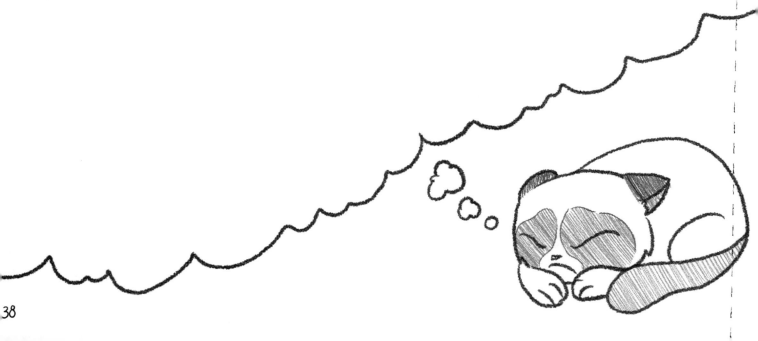

I'm running for PRESIDENT.
This is my grumpy
ACCEPTANCE SPEECH.

There are SO MANY THINGS that annoy me.
List your top five most
ANNOYING THINGS.

1. _____

2. _____

3. _____

4. _____

5. _____

What are your
TOP 3 TALENTS?

I doubt I'll be impressed.

1. _____

2. _____

3. _____

My talent is rolling my eyes.

I bet you have TERRIBLE taste in music.

What are your
FAVORITE 3 BANDS?

1. _____

2. _____

3. _____

Oh hey. I was right.

Draw a really boring
AMUSEMENT PARK RIDE
and give it a name.

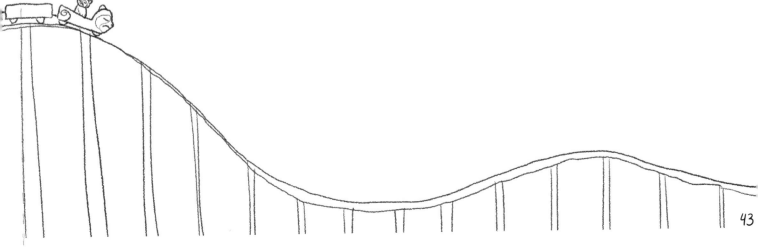

Blue boxes and old cars
make for TERRIBLE time machines.

Draw me a
COOLER TIME MACHINE.

Each year I go to in my time machine is EQUALLY UNIMPRESSIVE.

What YEAR would you go to?
Draw yourself in that year.

A lot of things make me FROWN.
What things
MAKE YOU GRUMPY?

Pokey says you should also write
things that make you HAPPY...

I DON'T SEE THE POINT.

A fun day for me is telling people
the COLD HARD TRUTH.

Draw what you would do on a "FUN" day.

NOPE.

Draw my CURRENT EXPRESSION based on my MOOD.

(I'll give you a hint. IT'S GRUMPY.)

The first thing I do when I wake up is GRUMBLE.

What is your
MORNING ROUTINE?

Draw yourself doing one of those activities.

We're superheroes... Design my AWESOME COSTUME and Pokey's less-awesome costume.

I WENT SHOPPING.
Nothing I bought made me happy.
What would YOU buy?

Drinking through NORMAL STRAWS is so DULL.

Draw me a better
TWISTY STRAW.

Pokey gave me this RIDICULOUS hat.
DRAW IT.

Design my grumpy
COMPUTER WALLPAPER.

Fill in the TOP 5 CONTACTS
that you wouldn't be too grumpy
about having on your PHONE.

How many WORDS can you
SPELL WITH MY NAME?

G   R   U   M   P   Y   C   A   T

The answer to GETTING UP in the morning is...

```
K E F E N F B R X S P I L P Y W Y O Y B
C J Z P T Y D W S K Z V O P L X J I O C
M F S O M B T L I R P T B L O L J J R Q
H W G N V H T N Q E S G U P A N D S O H
Q S E C W Q W T S W V Z H O B R N G X I
G L Q P M S Y A N G C J Y B M P C K P G
L R V S A C E L O Q D H I U M L Q O H U
S I E X N C V D S E E R E V E N B T R V
O C X E N J D V C X V O P G F D T S P C
V T M U V R E L Q Z I N X V I T Q I S W
N Z V U N X I Q W M T O J D Y R S S Y H
N U P Z E N B X W P A Z W I B D J E V V
A K L Y E D L I A T G D R O W S F D Z P
U G I L N O P L W N E Y A V D O N T F I
G F T Q Q H D X W U N I M W S W C P C I
```

NO (4 times)   NOPE   STOP   DON'T

NEVER   CEASE   DESIST   NEGATIVE

VOID   NULL   DECLINE

Circle all the words that
DESCRIBE ME.

TESTY	NONCHALANT
BLITHE	CROTCHETY
GROUCHY	CROSS
CHEERY	SPRIGHTLY
EFFERVESCENT	QUARRELSOME
HAPPY	WHIMSICAL
ORNERY	GLEEFUL
DOUR	SOUR
HIGH-SPIRITED	VINEGARY
JAUNTY	CHIPPER
PRICKLY	JOYFUL
MERRY	CRANKY

Fill out my
GRUMPY CROSSWORD.

ACROSS

3. My mouth can't do this
4. My common expression
6. All About _____ Me
8. Best part of a conversation

DOWN

1. My fur color
2. Easy way to turn someone down
4. Fancy word for cat
5. My negative response
7. My annoying counterpart
8. My classic trait
9. Pokey's fur color

UNSCRAMBLE these SUPER GRUMPY clue words.

Take the letters that appear in ⬭ boxes and unscramble them for the FINAL MESSAGE.

mewo

ocryguh

naykcr

wufla

eilorrhb

nlefie

pmurgy

oyodm

| M | | S | | | | | | | M | |

I'm going to a MASQUERADE.
DRAW ME A MASK.
Just don't make it too happy.

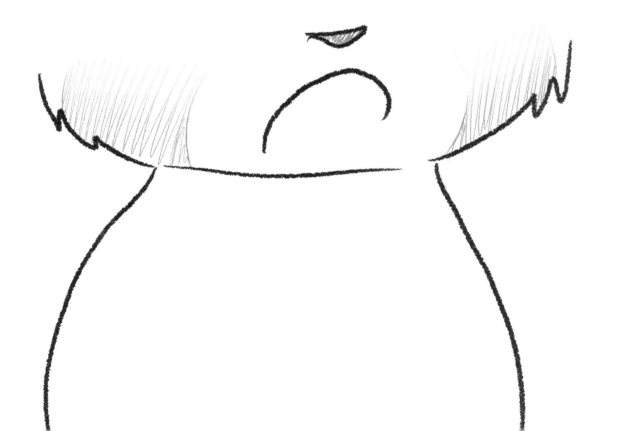

Solutions

The answer to GETTING UP in the morning is...

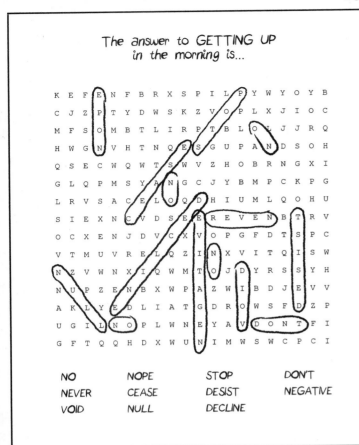

```
K E F E N F B R X S P I L P Y W Y O Y B
C J Z P T Y D W S K Z V O P L X J I O C
M F S O M B T L I R P T B L O L J J R Q
H W G N V H T N Q E S G U P A N D S O H
Q S E C W Q W T S W V Z H O B R N G X I
G L Q P M S Y A N G C J Y B M P C K P G
L R V S A C E L O Q D H I U M L Q O H U
S I E X N C V D S E E R E V E N B T R V
O C X E N J D V C X V O P G F D T S P C
V T M U V R E L Q Z I N X V I T Q I S W
N Z V W N X I Q W M T O J D Y R S S Y H
N U P Z E N B X W P A Z W I B D J E V V
A K L Y E D L I A T G D R O W S F D Z P
U G I L N O P L W N E Y A V D O N T F I
G F T Q Q H D X W U N I M W S W C P C I
```

NO	NOPE	STOP	DON'T
NEVER	CEASE	DESIST	NEGATIVE
VOID	NULL	DECLINE	

page 57

Circle all the words that DESCRIBE ME.

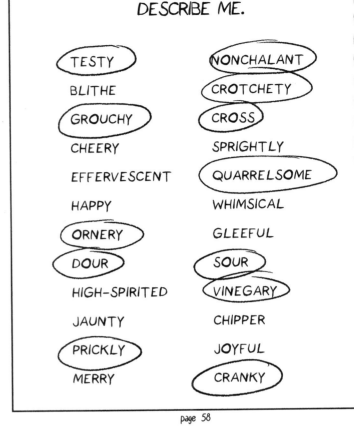

TESTY — NONCHALANT
BLITHE — CROTCHETY
GROUCHY — CROSS
CHEERY — SPRIGHTLY
EFFERVESCENT — QUARRELSOME
HAPPY — WHIMSICAL
ORNERY — GLEEFUL
DOUR — SOUR
HIGH-SPIRITED — VINEGARY
JAUNTY — CHIPPER
PRICKLY — JOYFUL
MERRY — CRANKY

page 58

Fill out my GRUMPY CROSSWORD.

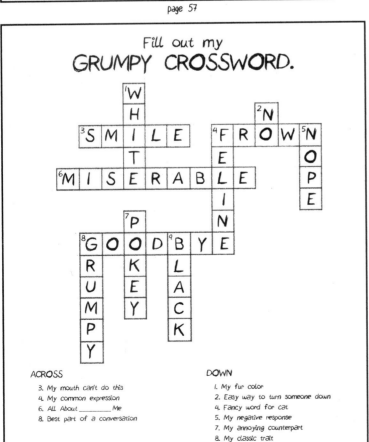

ACROSS
3. My mouth can't do this
4. My common expression
6. All About _____ Me
8. Best part of a conversation

DOWN
1. My fur color
2. Easy way to turn someone down
4. Fancy word for cat
5. My negative response
7. My annoying counterpart
8. My classic trait
9. Pokey's fur color

page 59

UNSCRAMBLE these SUPER GRUMPY clue words.

Take the letters that appear in ☐ boxes and unscramble them for the FINAL MESSAGE.

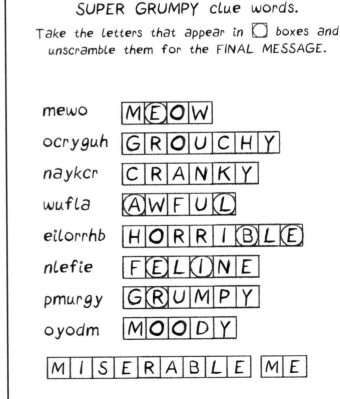

mewo — M E O W
ocryguh — G R O U C H Y
naykcr — C R A N K Y
wufla — A W F U L
eilorrhb — H O R R I B L E
nlefie — F E L I N E
pmurgy — G R U M P Y
oyodm — M O O D Y

M I S E R A B L E   M E

page 60